Make to Market

Planning the journey from craftsman to entrepreneur

Designed by Kathy Humenik
It's Worth Repeating

https://Itsworthrepeating.com

Make It To Market

Planning the journey from craftsman to entrepreneur

Written by

_____

Journals designed by It's Worth Repeating are created to capture some of your best memories or great ideas. Each journal is a small slice of your story, waiting for you to complete the details.

Titles include:

Strike Up the Band
Simply the Best
It's All Relative
Going to the Dogs
What's Cooking?
When I was a Kid
Back to Nature
This and That
And more.....

The journal collection can be found
 at our website: https://Itsworthrepeating.com

All of our journals are available for purchase on Amazon.com. Simply search "it's worth repeating" under books.

Make it to Market

From "Make it to Market" offers some intriguing background, useful tips, and journal space to capture your own ideas and plans for entering the often challenging, but seldom boring, world of craft fairs, festivals and farmer's markets.

This pursuit blends the spirit of an artist with the ambition of an entrepreneur. Those that are successful put their heart into the product and their head into the business of selling.

To begin with, participants are fiercely independent. They enjoy owning the process from beginning to end. They are adventurous. Travelling to new venues and engaging with new people week after week is definitely one adventure after another. And they are resilient. It's not always easy being responsible for everything and occasional fails are part of the game.

If the prosect is appealing, then the next big question is how to do it. In this book you will find a little information and hopefully some inspiration to get you started.

Make it to Market

Getting Started

What to Sell
    choosing a product
    setting a price

Where to Sell—finding the right venue

Setting the Stage
    Be prepared
    the Set-Up

Show time

For the Record

Unprompted

Getting Started

Begin at the beginning, and then go on until you come to the end.

Lewis Carroll

Getting Started

Crafting and craft markets have been with us for centuries. Today, markets and fairs are a thriving part of the community. They provide both a social experience and a venue for small-time entrepreneurs to establish a bona-fide business.

Crafting in many forms and flavors is alive and well in the United States. According to Statista over 25% of U.S. residents participate in some kind of art or craft activity.

The market research group, IMARC, indicates that the handicraft market in the United States reached over $260 billion in 2022. Indicating that many of those hobbyists have successfully navigated the route from make it to market.

If you are "craft minded" there is no shortage of ways to express your creative side in the marketplace.

Visit a busy craft marketplace and you will see everything including gallery quality art, hand-sewn apparel, restored vintage pieces and one-of-a-kind jewelry.

Getting Started

Markets themselves come in many flavors. There are art festivals that are often juried events, with stringent entry requirements. There are craft markets which primarily feature custom designed, hand-made items.

There are also flea markets and vintage fairs which focus on reclaimed and repurposed stock. And there are farmers' markets that often have locally crafted items in addition to fresh food and home-made edibles.

There are innumerable local markets held across the country. In addition to the ever- changing selection of craft fairs, there are over 8000 Farmers Markets recognized by the USDA and over 5000 registered flea markets.

Given the choice of product and the choice of venue where do you begin? How do you decide where and what to sell?

Getting Started

Let's start with a couple of questions to give the journey a little direction.

Perhaps the most important question of all is why do you want to enter the world of craft markets? Listed below are a few reasons why people participate.

Looking to make some extra money

Want recognition for my creativity

My hobby inventory is taking over my house

I'd like to meet some new people

My primary reason is:
_____

_____

_____

_____

If you have at least an idea of "why" than you have a place to begin

What to Sell

Every artist was first an amateur.

Ralph Waldo Emerson

What to Sell

You already have a few ideas about why you might like to sell. If your primary purpose is to gain attention for your skill and artistry as a crafter than you may have crafts that you have been involved with for a long time.

But if you are searching for the right product to sell because you are looking at this as a small business venture popular categories of crafted products include:

Fabric work: it can include custom prints, clothing, and home décor items. The final product is often a blend of texture, color, design and purpose.

Pottery and ceramic work is another well-represented field at craft shows. This includes hand-thrown bowls and plates, vases and wall décor.

Today resin products are popular with unique cutting boards, coasters and jewelry on display.

Personal use items include scented candles, hand-made jewelry, and skin-care products and are well represented at craft fairs.

What to Sell

There are often printed and paper items such as greeting cards, journals, and books. Home made food products can include sauces, candy, jams and various snack foods.

And products targeted to a specific demographic can do well. Homemade dog treats, dog beds, collars and tags are well received.

Bridal fairs have a niche appeal as do holiday themed items such as Christmas or Valentines day.

There are several web sites that offer an opinion on top selling craft products. According to the Made Urban blog the following are the top selling categories at craft fairs:

- Jewelry
- Art
- Photography
- Soap
- Candles
- Sewing

What to Sell

In addition to the tradition craft fair offerings, an area gaining popularity is salvaged and repurposed pieces and/or material. Entire fairs are sometimes dedicated to 'vintage." This can include reclaimed pieces that are offered for sale in all their tarnished glory.

It can also include items that have been enhanced or repurposed by the craftsman to increase their value. Furniture, clothing, tools, and general memorabilia fit this niche.

One other category that is sometimes available at craft fairs is "direct sales" items. These are commercially produced items made available to individuals for resale. Products include Scentsy, Mary Kay and Tupperware as examples. Most events limit this participation to ensure that the venue retains a feel of hand-crafted and artisan wares.

What to Sell

As a lover of crafts and craft markets there have no doubt been some items that have made an impression on you.

What is a piece of work that really stood out for you? Why did it make such an impression?

_____

_____

_____

_____

_____

What is one of the strangest things you've seen at a craft market? Did you love it or hate it?

_____

_____

_____

_____

_____

What to Sell

What kind of products are most likely to attract your attention?

_____

_____

_____

_____

_____

What items do you have little or no interest in?

_____

_____

_____

_____

_____

What to Sell

So how do you decide what to pursue? You have some ideas about what you like and what you don't like.

Starting with the obvious, is there a hobby or craft that you are interested in? If the answer is yes, then the next questions would be how marketable is your hand-crafted item? Will it have broad appeal or is your intent to bring one-of-a-kind pieces to market that stand out for their originality? One way to gain some insight on this is to peruse on-line sites like Etsy and Shopify.

Attending a few craft fairs as a potential participant offers valuable perspective. Talk to the vendors and find out what kind of feedback they get; what sells and why. You'll be surprised at how willing people are to share their experiences.

Pay attention to the booths that are busy. What seems to attract customers? Is the craft offered particularly unique, cute, quirky or just priced right?

If you are more interested in the busines side of things understanding what sells and why is a crucial part of your decision.

What to Sell

Once you narrow down the list of your potential products, some work needs to go into understanding the business proposition at hand.

If you have decided you are entering the marketplace to gain attention to your craft, or simply for the fun of the experience you may just want to recover your costs. But if you are trying to actually create an income, then the numbers need to be a little different.

So how do you price your item? Like everything for sale, there are basically two components, what it costs and what it is worth to the buyer. Pricing based on your costs is commonly called cost-based pricing. Pricing based on what you think a buyer will pay is market-based pricing.

With cost-based pricing, the approach is to calculate total costs associated with the item, determine the profit ratio you desire, and establish a target price.

Market-based pricing looks at numbers from the view of the buyer. What would they see as the value of your item? What do comparable products sell for? In this case your costs are secondary to what the market will determine your item is worth.

What to Sell

A simple approach to calculating product costs is to break costs into two categories; direct material costs and overhead or indirect dollars.

Direct costs include money spent to procure material that is incorporated into an item. For example, if you make candles, direct cost could include wax, scents, wicks and containers or base. Paid labor associated with product creation should be captured also. Packaging could also be considered a direct cost.

Indirect costs might include your vendor fees, transportation costs, marketing material (like website fees) tools etc. Because indirect costs are not linked specifically to an individual item, these costs can be pro-rated across sales.

This approach is fairly straight forward and allows you to capture the total cost of your endeavor.

It is likely that there will be some estimating in your process but over time you can refine the numbers to gain a good understanding of total cost and what you are actually earning.

A simple example of how to capture costs

The product I am offering for sale is

_____

Costs:

Material a:_____ cost per unit_____

Material b:_____ cost per unit_____

Material c:_____ cost per unit_____

Total direct costs:_____

Overhead:

Vendor fees:_____

Marketing:_____

Licenses:_____

Insurance:_____

Total direct costs per item:

_____

Overhead allocation per item:

_____

Break even price point:

_____

Desired profit percentage:_____

Product sales price:_____

So, if your candle cost five dollars to produce, carried a dollar per item as overhead and you hoped to make 25% per item, you would need to sell it for $7.50

This may sound more complicated than necessary and in fact much of the costs, especially the overhead, end up being estimates, but going through the thought process is valuable. It's easy to think you are making money when in fact you are not. If you are in it for the fun, great! But if you are in it to produce an income, knowing the numbers is a must.

Below are links to a few nationwide craft associations. They offer both information and community around the crafting industry

Craft Industry Alliance
https://craftindustryalliance.org/

Society of Arts and Crafts
https://societyofcrafts.org/

If you are interested in more data regarding the crafting industry, check out Statists

Statista

https://www.statista.com/topics/3908/crafts-and-creative-activities-in-the-united-states/#topicOverview

What to Sell

Connecting with like minded artists and sellers can create a valuable network. What are some organizations you wish to investigate?

Crafting Organizations of interest:

Name: Contact Info:

_____

_____

_____

_____

_____

_____

_____

_____

What to Sell

Individual crafters and vendors to connect with:

Name: Contact Info:

_____

_____

_____

_____

_____

_____

_____

_____

_____

_____

_____

_____

Where to Sell

The right product at the right place with the right price makes the sale.

anonymous

Where to Sell

Knowing what to sell and knowing what to sell it for, are two important pieces of the puzzle, but knowing where to sell is equally important.

Matching the venue with what you are offering for sale is one key to a successful outcome. Just like retail storefronts, craft markets and festivals may have a particular customer set that they are appealing to. To illustrate the point, bringing pet products to a bridal fair or meat products to an event for vegans is likely to result in poor sales.

You get the idea. Markets often have themes and it's important that your products fit in.

Another key criteria is location. Or as they say, "location, location, location." Is the venue assessable for many potential shoppers? Is there ample parking for customers and vendors alike? Is the general locale of the event inviting?

You may also what to consider the promotion undertaken for the event itself. Is there good advertising? Is there a social media presence that garners attention? Is the event affiliated with other popular community activities? Basically, will people hear about it and be interested in attending?

Where to Sell

With that information you can decide if the event is right for you and if it is worth the vendor fee you will pay to participate.

Booth fees can be under $50 for a local school or church event. Farmers' markets are generally under $100 for participation as well.

Booth fees for a good size show (75+ vendors) can range from $100-$200 and more depending on show length. Large trade shows with hundreds of vendors can be considerably more.

In addition to booth fees, some shows charge an application fee and may also expect you to have liability insurance and appropriate local licenses; all part of the cost of participation. Make sure when you are considering a show that you understand all your financial obligations.

Where to Sell

There are several ways to find out what the sales opportunities are in your area. A good starting point is to join a network of other crafters. Social media makes it easy to find fellow artists and sellers.

Also check out regional/county news pages and bulletins that announce upcoming events. There are several sites that specialize in information regarding festivals and arts and crafts shows. They can generally be searched by location and/or dates. A little "googling" will easily find them for your area.

And don't forget to ask your network of friends and family about events that they may be familiar with like school or church fund-raisers.

How are you finding potential marketplaces for your product? Websites? Contacts?

_____

_____

_____

_____

What is the general locale that you wish to sell in?

_____

_____

_____

_____

_____

_____

_____

What is most important to you about the venue that you sell at?

_____

_____

_____

_____

_____

What would keep you from selling at a certain location or show?

_____

_____

_____

_____

_____

_____

_____

Craft shows across the country come in all flavors. Here are some links to sites that claim to know the best of the best shows.

Best Craft Fairs
https://bestcraftfairs.com/

Trade Fest
https://tradefest.io/en/tag/arts-and-crafts

Festival.net
https://festivalnet.com/

Arts and Crafts Show Yellow Pages
http://www.craftshowyellowpages.com/

Where to Sell

Shows and Markets of interest:

Name: Contact Info:

_____

_____

_____

_____

_____

_____

_____

_____

_____

_____

_____

_____

Where to Sell

Other resources to identify market opportunities:

Name: Contact Info:

_____

_____

_____

_____

_____

_____

_____

_____

_____

_____

_____

_____

Setting the Stage

A beautiful display is the icing on the cake.

Setting the Stage

You have decided what you are going to sell and where you are going to sell it. It's time to get ready for the show.

An attractive, composed display is one of the most important things you can do to enhance your sales.

Building the space

Outside shows will often require tents or awnings and may specify the color as well. Make sure that you select a sturdy product in good repair, including necessary weights to prevent your "store" from flying away in the wind. Even with an inside space you may choose to set up an awning as a way of delineating your sales area.

Display Hardware

Tables, shelves and racks are the staples for displaying your wares. They are available at several on-line suppliers as well as in local hardware and variety stores. Some vendors use crates, boxes and cabinets for display, and these can add charm to your booth. Everything needs to be sturdy and reliable. Tables should be covered to the floor. (In addition to looking attractive, you create a hidden space for extra inventory.)

Setting the Stage

Product Placement

When you assemble your "storefront" make sure that what you are selling is easily accessible to the buyer. Don't block shelves and tables with your chairs or cash register.

Try to create height in your display so that products are at eye level and can catch the buyers' attention.

Signage

Make sure that your business name is easy to see. Printed banners, flyers and other signage is a small investment to be recognized and to look professional. Have prices or price-lists readily available so that customers don't have to ask.

De-clutter

It may be tempting to have as much variety as possible on display but don't overwhelm your set-up. Too much of a good thing looks chaotic and unprofessional and can be very distracting.

Setting the Stage

There are a few things to have for your show besides good product and good displays. It's easy to forget the small things that can help make your show successful. Review the following checklist for additional items to have on hand.

Adequate cash/change

Credit card processing supplies

Apron or small accessory container

Pens

Price Tags

Business Cards

Contact Information for custom orders

Tape and extra display hooks

Bags or boxes for product take away

Wipes or tissues

Showtime

Success is the sum of all small efforts repeated, again and again.

Showtime

Your set-up is complete. Your product is on display, and you are ready to greet your customers. Smiling and saying hello is the most important step you can take. You don't need to overwhelm people that are passing by but be welcoming. Make eye contact and encourage conversation.

If they seem interested in a particular item share the background. People love the stories that go with their purchase.

Were you inspired to create because of a certain experience in your life? How did you acquire the skill to design and make your product? What makes your offering special?

Stay in character. Be professional and engaged. Many vendors have lost sales because of disconnecting from the event. Limit both cell phone usage and snacking.

Most importantly, have fun. That is the biggest benefit of participating. You meet new people, you receive feedback on your work, and you gain new ideas for the next event.

Showtime

During the day, keep your display fresh. Add new inventory and fill in the spaces when product sells.

If you have a partner to watch your booth, take some time to walk through the event and connect with other vendors. See what is generating interest and who/what might be floundering.

Because each show is different, with its own vibe, don't be discouraged if you aren't selling as much as you would like. Just pay attention to the type of crowd and inventory to give you insight for your next show selection.

Keep smiling and positive. Wait until the show closes to break down your booth. That is considerate of the customers, other vendors and the show organizer.

And remember, whether you sold a little or a lot, you had an experience to enjoy and learn from.

What factors do you consider when deciding if an event was successful?

For the Record

It never hurts to write things down.

For the Record

Being intentional about moving forward can help you plan for success. The following pages are an opportunity to build a simple plan for a few shows and to record the outcome of each event. This doesn't have to be complicated, but you will be surprised at how helpful it is to right down all those great ideas.

Recording the good and the bad of a show leads to improvements for the next event.

Selling is a skill that improves with practice. Learning what works for you is going to help you learn what works for the customers as well.

Have fun and be patient. Selling, just like crafting, is an art.

Where have you identified as possible sales locations?

Event	Location

Date	Fee

Event	Location

Date	Fee

Event	Location

Date	Fee

For the Record

For the record—show one at:

_____

Show One: _____

I chose this show because:

_____
_____
_____
_____
_____

At this show I plan to sale primarily:

_____
_____
_____
_____
_____
_____
_____

Show One: _____

The biggest challenge with this show will be:

_____

_____

_____

_____

_____

_____

_____

_____

_____

_____

Show One—the results

My total sales were:

_____

_____

_____

_____

The items that sold best were:

_____

_____

_____

_____

My net profit was about:

_____

_____

_____

Show One – the results

The highlight of this show for me was:

_____

_____

_____

_____

_____

_____

_____

_____

_____

_____

Show One – the results

At the next show I will continue to:

_____

_____

_____

_____

_____

_____

_____

_____

_____

Show One – the results

At the next show the changes I will make are:

_____

_____

_____

_____

_____

_____

_____

_____

_____

_____

_____

For the Record

For the record—show two at:

_____

Show Two: _____

I chose this show because:

_____
_____
_____
_____
_____

At this show I plan to sale primarily:

_____
_____
_____
_____
_____
_____
_____

Show Two: _____

The biggest challenge with this show will be:

_____

_____

_____

_____

_____

_____

_____

_____

_____

_____

Show Two—the results

My total sales were:

_____

_____

_____

_____

The items that sold best were:

_____

_____

_____

_____

My net profit was about:

_____

_____

_____

_____

Show Two – the results

The highlight of this show for me was:

_____

_____

_____

_____

_____

_____

_____

_____

_____

Show Two – the results

At the next show I will continue to:

Show Two – the results

At the next show the changes I will make are:

_____

_____

_____

_____

_____

_____

_____

_____

_____

_____

_____

_____

For the Record

For the record—show three at:

_____

Show Three:
_____

I chose this show because:
_____
_____
_____
_____
_____

At this show I plan to sale primarily:
_____
_____
_____
_____
_____
_____
_____

Show Three: _____

The biggest challenge with this show will be:

_____

_____

_____

_____

_____

_____

_____

_____

_____

_____

Show Three—the results

My total sales were:

_____

_____

_____

_____

The items that sold best were:

_____

_____

_____

_____

My net profit was about:

_____

_____

_____

_____

Show Three – the results

The highlight of this show for me was:

_____

_____

_____

_____

_____

_____

_____

_____

_____

_____

Show Three– the results

At the next show I will continue to:

_____

_____

_____

_____

_____

_____

_____

_____

_____

_____

_____

Show Three – the results

At the next show the changes I will make are:

_____

_____

_____

_____

_____

_____

_____

_____

_____

_____

_____

Closing Thoughts

You've learned something about your craft, something about selling and something about yourself.

And you put your best foot forward. No doubt there were some wins and some losses, but remember what Mark Twain said:

"Twenty years from now you will be more disappointed by the things that you didn't do than by what you have done."

Each experience leads us to the next. If you are an entrepreneur at heart, there are many great experiences yet to come. Enjoy the journey and craft on.

Unprompted

More stories, ideas and opinions worthy of sharing

More stories, ideas and opinions worthy of sharing

More stories, ideas and opinions worthy of sharing

More stories, ideas and opinions worthy of sharing

More stories, ideas and opinions worthy of sharing

Printed in Great Britain
by Amazon

IMMIGRATION CONTROL IN A WARMING WORLD

REALIZING THE MORAL CHALLENGES OF CLIMATE MIGRATION

Johannes Graf Keyserlingk

ia

imprint-academic.com

Copyright © Johannes Graf Keyserlingk, 2018

The moral rights of the authors have been asserted.
No part of this publication may be reproduced in any form
without permission, except for the quotation of brief passages
in criticism and discussion.

Published in the UK by
Imprint Academic, PO Box 200, Exeter EX5 5YX, UK

Distributed in the USA by
Ingram Book Company,
One Ingram Blvd., La Vergne, TN 37086, USA

ISBN 9781845409791

A CIP catalogue record for this book is available from the
British Library and US Library of Congress